Important Inst

Students, Parents, and Teachers can use the URL or QR code provided below to access Lumos back to school refresher online assessment. Please note that this assessment is provided in the Online format only.

URL
Visit the URL below and place the book access code **http://www.lumoslearning.com/a/tedbooks** **Access Code: BS56M-12379-P**
OR **Scan the QR code with your Smartphone** 

Lumos Learning
Developed by Expert Teachers

Lumos Back-to-School Refresher tedBook - Grade 6 Math, Back to School book to address Summer Slide designed for classroom and home use

Contributing Author   - April LoTempio
Executive Producer   - Mukunda Krishnaswamy
Designer and Illustrator - Devraj Dharmaraj

First Edition - 2020

ISBN-13: 978-1-081937-30-0

Printed in the United States of America

For permissions and additional information contact us

Lumos Information Services, LLC
PO Box 1575, Piscataway, NJ 08855-1575
http://www.LumosLearning.com

Email: support@lumoslearning.com
Tel: (732) 384-0146
Fax: (866) 283-6471

Developed by Expert Teachers

Table of Contents

INTRODUCTION

This book is specifically designed to help diagnose and remedy Summer Learning Loss in students who are starting their sixth grade classes. It provides a comprehensive and efficient review of 5th Grade Math standards through an online assessment. Before starting sixth grade instruction, parents/teachers can administer this online test to their students. After the students complete the test, a standards mastery report is immediately generated to pinpoint any proficiency gaps. Using the diagnostic report and the accompanying study plan, students can get targeted remedial practice through lessons included in this book to overcome any Summer learning loss.

Addressing the Summer slide during the first few weeks of a new academic will help students have a productive sixth grade experience.

The online program also gives your student an opportunity to briefly explore various standards that are included in the 6th grade curriculum.

Some facts about Summer Learning Loss
- Students often lose an average of 2 and ½ months of math skills
- Students often lose 2 months of reading skills
- Teachers spend at least the first 4 to 5 weeks of the new school year reteaching important skills and concepts

Lumos Learning Back-To-School Refresher Methodology
The following graphic shows the key components of the Lumos back-to-school refresher program.

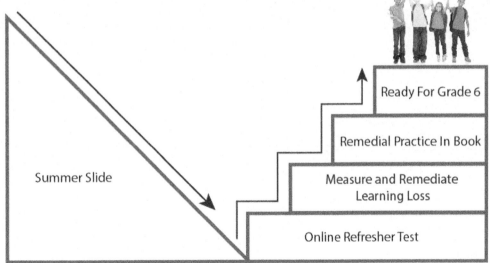

Summer Slide

Ready For Grade 6

Remedial Practice In Book

Measure and Remediate Learning Loss

Online Refresher Test

Chapter 1
Assess Summer Learning Loss

Step 1: Assess Online Diagnostic Assessment

Use the URL and access code provided below or scan the QR code to access the Diagnostic assessment and get started. The online diagnostic test helps to measure the summer loss and remediate loss in an efficient and effective way.

After completing the test, your student will receive immediate feedback with detailed reports on standards mastery. With this report, use the next section of the book to design a practice plan for your student to overcome the summer loss.

URL	QR Code
Visit the URL below and place the book access code **http://www.lumoslearning.com/a/tedbooks** **Access Code: BS56M-12379-P**	

Step 2: Review the Personalized Study Plan Online

After you complete the online practice test, access your individualized study plan from the table of contents (Figure 2)

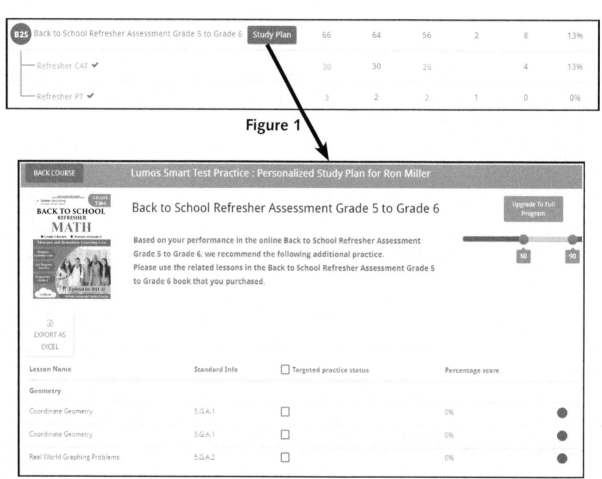

Figure 1

Figure 2

Step 3: Remediate Summer Learning Loss

Using the information provided in the study plan report, complete the targeted practice using the appropriate lessons in this book to overcome Summer learning loss. Using the Lesson Name, find the appropriate practice lessons in this book and answer the questions provided. After completing the practice in the book you can mark the progress in your study plan as shown the figure 2. Please use the answer key and detailed answers provided for each lesson to gain further understanding of the learning objective.

Operations and Algebraic Thinking

5.OA.A.1 Write and Interpret Numerical Expressions & Patterns

1. Evaluate the expression (8 x 6) + (8-3)?

   Ⓐ 53
   Ⓑ 48
   Ⓒ 64
   Ⓓ 81

2. Where must the parenthesis be in the following expression so that the answer is 6?

   20 - 8 ÷ 2

   Ⓐ 20 - (8 ÷ 2)
   Ⓑ (20 - 8) ÷ 2

3. Evaluate the expression 4 x (2 + 1) + 6.

   Ⓐ 18
   Ⓑ 15
   Ⓒ 21
   Ⓓ 16

4. What is the value of 2 x [5-(6 ÷3)]?

5.OA.A.2 Record and Interpret Calculations with Numbers

1. Olivia had 42 pieces of candy. She kept 9 pieces for herself and then divided the rest evenly among her three friends. Which expression best represents the number of candy each friend received?

   Ⓐ (42 ÷ 3) - 9
   Ⓑ (42 − 9) ÷ 3
   Ⓒ 42 ÷ (9 − 3)
   Ⓓ 42 − (9 ÷ 3)

2. Which is true about the solution to 8 x (467 + 509)?

   Ⓐ It is a number in the ten thousands.
   Ⓑ It is an odd number.
   Ⓒ It is eight times greater than the sum of 467 and 509.
   Ⓓ It is 509 more than the product of 8 and 467.

3. Which is true about the solution to (3,259 − 741) ÷ 3?

   Ⓐ It is one third as much as the difference between 3,259 and 741.
   Ⓑ It is 741 less than the quotient of 3,259 divided by 3.
   Ⓒ It is a whole number.
   Ⓓ It is a number in the thousands.

4. **Part A**
   Which of these expressions would result in the greatest number?

   Ⓐ 420 − (28 x 13)
   Ⓑ 420 + 28 + 13
   Ⓒ (420 − 28) x 13
   Ⓓ 420 + (28 x 13)

   Part B
   Which of these expressions would result in the smallest number?

   Ⓐ 684 − (47 + 6)
   Ⓑ 684 − 47 − 6
   Ⓒ (684 − 47) x 6
   Ⓓ 684 − (47 x 6)

5.OA.B.3 Analyze Patterns and Relationships

1. **Which set of numbers completes the function table?**
    Rule: subtract 4

Input	Output
☐	1
7	3
☐	7
☐	10
☐	15

    Ⓐ 0, 3, 6, 11
    Ⓑ 3, 10, 17, 25
    Ⓒ 4, 28, 40, 60
    Ⓓ 5, 11, 14, 19

2. **Which set of numbers completes the function table?**
    Rule: add 1, then multiply by 5

Input	Output
☐	5
2	15
☐	20
☐	35
☐	55

    Ⓐ 2, 5, 15, 20
    Ⓑ 1, 4, 7, 11
    Ⓒ 30, 105, 180, 280
    Ⓓ 0, 3, 6, 10

3. **Which rule describes the function table?**

x	y
11	5
14	8
21	15
28	22

Ⓐ Add 3
Ⓑ Subtract 6
Ⓒ Subtract 1, then divide by 2
Ⓓ Divide by 2, Add 1

4. **Which rule describes the function table?**

x	y
4	4
7	10
13	22
20	36

Ⓐ Multiply by 2, then subtract 4
Ⓑ Add zero
Ⓒ Add 3
Ⓓ Subtract 1, then multiply by 2

5. **Consider the following pattern:**
    7, 9, 4, 6, 1, . . .
    If the pattern continued, what would be the first negative number to appear?
    Write your answer in the box given below.

Operations and Algebraic Thinking

Answer Key
&
Detailed Explanations

5.OA.A.1 Write and Interpret Numerical Expressions & Patterns

Question No.	Answer	Detailed Explanations
1	A	First, evaluate the numbers within brackets 8 x 6 = 48; 8 -3 = 5 Now, in step 2, add both the numbers. 48 + 5 = 53. Hence, A is the correct answer choice.
2	B	Choice A will be 20 - 4 = 16, while choice b is 12 ÷ 2 = 6. Hence, B is the correct answer choice.
3	A	4 x (2 + 1) + 6 = 4 x 3 + 6 = 12 + 6 = 18 which is the correct answer. Hence, answer choice A is correct.
4	6	When working with parentheses ( ) and brackets [ ], work from the inside to the outside. First solve the expression in the parentheses. 2 x [5 - (6 ÷ 3)] = 2 x [5 - (2)] Next solve the expression in the brackets. 2 x [5 - (2)] = 2 x [3] Finally, solve the resulting expression. 2 x [3] = 6

5.OA.A.2 Record and Interpret Calculations with Numbers

Question No.	Answer	Detailed Explanations
1	B	First, subtract the 9 that Olivia kept for herself (42 – 9). Then divide the difference among the three friends: (42 – 9) ÷ 3.
2	C	The expression 8 x (467 + 509) indicates that you should first find the sum of 467 and 509, and then multiply by 8. Therefore, the solution is 8 times greater than that sum.
3	A	The expression (3,259 – 741) ÷ 3 indicates that you should first find the difference of 3,259 and 741, and then divide by 3. Therefore, the solution is one third as much as that difference.
4 Part A	C	A quick estimate shows that option C, a number in the hundreds times a number in the tens, would result in a number in the thousands. The other options would all result in a number in the hundreds.
4 Part B	D	A quick estimate shows that option D, in which the largest amount is subtracted from 684, would result in the smallest number. Options A and B subtract a relatively small amount from 684, and option C will actually result in a larger number.

5.OA.B.3 Analyze Patterns and Relationships

Question No.	Answer	Detailed Explanations
1	D	The rule is -4, Option (A) is incorrect. because 0 -4 = -4 and not 1. (If the rule does not work for one number, we need not check for other numbers). Option (B) is incorrect, because 3 - 4 = -1 and not 1. Option (C) is incorrect, because 4 - 4 = 0 and not 1. All the numbers in option (D) satisfies the rule. $5 - 4 = 1, 11 - 4 = 7, 14 - 4 = 10, 19 - 4 = 15$
2	D	The rule is +1, x5, Option (A) is incorrect, because (2 + 1) x 5 = 15 not 5. (If the rule does not work for one number, we need not check for other numbers). Option (B) is incorrect, because (1 + 1) x 5 =10 not 5 Option (C) is incorrect, because (30 + 1) x 5 = 155 not 5 All the numbers in option (D) satisfies the rule. $(0 + 1) \times 5 = 5, (3 + 1) \times 5 = 20, (6 + 1) \times 5 = 35, (10 + 1) \times 5 = 55.$
3	B	Option (A) is incorrect, because 11 + 3 = 14 NOT 5. Option (B) is correct, as subtracting 6 from each x-value results in the corresponding y-value as follows: $11 - 6 = 5, 14 - 6 = 8, 21 - 6 = 15, 28 - 6 = 22.$ Note that, once we get the correct option, we need not check other options.
4	A	Option (A) is correct because multiplying each x-value by 2 and then subtracting 4 results in the corresponding y-value as follows: $4 \times 2 - 4 = 4, 7 \times 2 - 4 = 10, 13 \times 2 - 4 = 22, 20 \times 2 - 4 = 36.$ Note that, once we get the correct option, we need not check other options.
5	-2	The pattern is Add 2, Subtract 5. Since 5 was just subtracted from 6 to get 1, the pattern would continue: 3, -2 . . .

Number & Operations
in Base Ten

5.NBT.A.1 Place Value

1. **What is the equivalent of 4 and 3/100?**

    Ⓐ 40.3
    Ⓑ 0.403
    Ⓒ 4.03
    Ⓓ 403.0

2. **In the number 16,428,095 what is the value of the digit 6?**

    Ⓐ 6 million
    Ⓑ 60 thousand
    Ⓒ 60 million
    Ⓓ 600 thousand

3. **What is the value of 9 in the number 5,802.109**

    Ⓐ 9 thousand
    Ⓑ 9 tenths
    Ⓒ 9 thousandths
    Ⓓ 9 hundredths

4. **Which comparison is correct?**

    Ⓐ 50.5 = 50.05
    Ⓑ 0.05 = 0.50
    Ⓒ 0.005 = 500.0
    Ⓓ 0.50 = 0.500

5. **The place value of the digit 3 in 67.039 is _____.**
    Fill in the blank

5.NBT.A.2 Multiplication & Division of Powers of Ten

1. **Astronomers calculate a distant star to be 3 x 10^5 light years away. How far away is the star?**

   Ⓐ 30,000 light years
   Ⓑ 3,000 light years
   Ⓒ 3,000,000 light years
   Ⓓ 300,000 light years

2. **A scientist calculates the weight of a substance as 6.9 ÷ 10^4 grams. What is the weight of the substance?**

   Ⓐ 69,000 grams
   Ⓑ 69 milligrams
   Ⓒ 0.00069 grams
   Ⓓ 6.9 kilograms

3. **Looking through a microscope, a doctor finds a germ that is 0.00000082 millimeters long. How can he write this number in his notes?**

   Ⓐ 8.2×10^7
   Ⓑ $8.2 \div 10^7$
   Ⓒ $8.2 \times 10^{0.00001}$
   Ⓓ $8.2 \div 700$

4. **Which of the following is 10^5 times greater than 0.016?**

   Ⓐ 160
   Ⓑ 1,600
   Ⓒ 16.0
   Ⓓ 1.60

5. **Write the number 1,000 as a power of ten. Enter your answer in the box given below**

5.NBT.A.3.A Read and Write Decimals

1. **The number 0.05 can be represented by which fraction?**

    Ⓐ $\frac{0}{5}$

    Ⓑ $\frac{5}{100}$

    Ⓒ $\frac{5}{10}$

    Ⓓ $\frac{1}{05}$

2. **Which of the following numbers is equivalent to one half?**

    Ⓐ 0.2
    Ⓑ 0.12
    Ⓒ 1.2
    Ⓓ 0.5

3. **How is the number sixty three hundredths written?**

    Ⓐ 0.63
    Ⓑ 0.063
    Ⓒ 0.0063
    Ⓓ 6.300

4. **What is the correct way to read the number 40.057?**

    Ⓐ Forty point five seven
    Ⓑ Forty and fifty-seven hundredths
    Ⓒ Forty and fifty-seven thousandths
    Ⓓ Forty and five hundredths and seven thousandths

5. **What is the standard form of this number?**
    Seventy-nine million, four hundred seventeen thousand, six hundred eight
    Enter your answer in the box given below

    ```
    
    
    
    ```

5.NBT.A.3.B Comparing and Ordering Decimals

1. Arrange these numbers in order from greatest to least:
   2.4, 2.04, 2.21, 2.20

   Ⓐ 2.4, 2.04, 2.21, 2.20
   Ⓑ 2.4, 2.21, 2.20, 2.04
   Ⓒ 2.21, 2.20, 2.4, 2.04
   Ⓓ 2.20, 2.4, 2.04, 2.21

2. Which of the following numbers completes the sequence below?
   4.17, _____, 4.19

   Ⓐ 4.18
   Ⓑ 4.81
   Ⓒ 5.17
   Ⓓ 4.27

3. Which of the following comparisons is true?

   Ⓐ 0.403 > 0.304
   Ⓑ 0.043 < 0.403
   Ⓒ 0.043 < 0.304
   Ⓓ All of the above

4. Which number completes the following sequence?
   2.038, 2.039, _____

   Ⓐ 2.049
   Ⓑ 2.400
   Ⓒ 2.0391
   Ⓓ 2.04

5. Order the following numbers from least to greatest.
   1.003, 0.853, 0.85, 1.03, 0.96, 0.921
   Enter your answers in the correct order in the boxes given below

5.NBT.A.4 Rounding Decimals

1. Which of the following numbers would round to 13.75?

   Ⓐ 13.755
   Ⓑ 13.70
   Ⓒ 13.756
   Ⓓ 13.747

2. Jerry spent $5.91, $7.27, and $12.60 on breakfast, lunch, and dinner. Approximately how much did he spend on meals?

   Ⓐ about $24
   Ⓑ about $26
   Ⓒ about $25
   Ⓓ about $27

3. Maria needs to buy wood for a door frame. She needs two pieces that are 6.21 feet long and one piece that is 2.5 feet long. About how much wood should she buy?

   Ⓐ about 15 feet
   Ⓑ about 9 feet
   Ⓒ about 17 feet
   Ⓓ about 14 feet

4. Mika has a rectangular flower garden. It measures 12.2 meters on one side and 7.8 meters on the other. What is a reasonable estimation of the area of the flower garden? (Area= length x width)

   Ⓐ 96 square meters
   Ⓑ 20 square meters
   Ⓒ 66 square meters
   Ⓓ 120 square meters

5. Read each statement below and mark the correct column to indicate whether you must round up or keep the digit.

	Round Up	Keep
Round 5.483 to the nearest hundredth.		
Round 6.625 to the nearest tenth.		
Round 77.951 to the nearest one.		
Round 172.648 to the nearest hundredth.		

5.NBT.B.5 Multiplication of Whole Numbers

1. **Which equation is represented by this array?**

    Ⓐ 3 + 7 + 3 + 7 = 20
    Ⓑ 7 + 7 + 7 + 7 + 7 = 35
    Ⓒ 3 x 3 + 7 = 16
    Ⓓ 3 x 7 = 21

2. **What would be a quick way to solve 596 x 101 accurately?**

    Ⓐ Multiply 5 x 101, 9 x 101, 6 x 101, then add the products.
    Ⓑ Multiply 596 x 100 then add 596 more.
    Ⓒ Shift the 1 and multiply 597 x 100 instead.
    Ⓓ Estimate 600 x 100.

3. **Harold baked 9 trays of cookies for a party. Three of the trays held 15 cookies each and six of the trays held 18 cookies each. How many cookies did Harold bake in all?**

    Ⓐ 297
    Ⓑ 135
    Ⓒ 153
    Ⓓ 162

4. **Solve.**
    407 x 35 = _____

    Ⓐ 14,280
    Ⓑ 14,245
    Ⓒ 12,445
    Ⓓ 16,135

5. **What is the product of 321 X 1854**
    Enter your answer in the box given below.

5.NBT.B.6 Division of Whole Numbers

1. The fifth grade class took a field trip to the theater. The 96 students sat in rows with 10 students in each row. How many rows did they use?

   Ⓐ 11
   Ⓑ 9
   Ⓒ 10
   Ⓓ 12

2. What is the value of 6,720 ÷ 15?

   Ⓐ 510
   Ⓑ 426
   Ⓒ 448
   Ⓓ 528

3. What is 675,000 divided by 100?

   Ⓐ 675
   Ⓑ 67,500
   Ⓒ 67.5
   Ⓓ 6,750

4. Which of the following statements is true?

   Ⓐ 75 ÷ 0 = 0
   Ⓑ 75 ÷ 0 = 1
   Ⓒ 75 ÷ 0 = 75
   Ⓓ 75 ÷ 0 cannot be solved

5. Divide 388 by 15.
   Enter the answer in the box given below

5.NBT.B.7 Add, Subtract, Multiply, & Divide Decimals

1. Normal body temperature is 98.6 degrees Fahrenheit. When Tyler had a fever, his temperature went up to 102.2 degrees. By how much did Tyler's temperature increase?

   Ⓐ 4.4 degrees
   Ⓑ 3.6 degrees
   Ⓒ 4.2 degrees
   Ⓓ 3.2 degrees

2. A stamp costs $0.42. How much money would you need to buy 8 stamps?

   Ⓐ $.82
   Ⓑ $3.33
   Ⓒ $3.36
   Ⓓ $4.52

3. Find the product:
   0.25 x 1.1 =

   Ⓐ .75
   Ⓑ 0.275
   Ⓒ 0.27
   Ⓓ .25

4. Divide 0.42 by 3.

   Ⓐ 14
   Ⓑ 126
   Ⓒ 0.14
   Ⓓ 12.6

5. Solve:
   0.05 ÷ 0.2
   Enter your answer in the box below.

Numbers and Operations in Base Ten

Answer Key
&
Detailed Explanations

5.NBT.A.1 Place Value

Question No.	Answer	Detailed Explanations
1	C	Write the number 4 in the ones place. The word 'and' indicates the decimal point. The fractional part of the number is three-hundredths, which is shown with a 3 in the hundredths place. Use a placeholder 0 in the tenths place, so the 3 is two places to the right of the decimal.
2	A	The 6 is seven places to the left of the decimal, which is the millions place. Its value is 6 million.
3	C	The 9 is three places to the right of the decimal, which is the thousandths place. Its value is 9 thousandths.
4	D	In order for two numbers to be equal, they must have the same digits in the same place value. In this option, each number has a 5 in the tenths place. The final zeros after the tenths place do not change the value.
5	Hundredths	The first digit to the right of a decimal point is the tenths place. The next digit to the right is the hundredths place. The correct answer is hundredths because the 3 is two places to the right of the decimal

5.NBT.A.2 Multiplication & Division of Powers of Ten

Question No.	Answer	Detailed Explanations
1	D	10^5 means 10 x 10 x 10 x 10 x 10, which equals 100,000. 3 x 100,000 = 300,000. Another way to think of this problem is 3 x 10 = 30, then make sure the number of zeros in the answer matches the number of the exponent (5), which is 300,000.
2	C	10^4 means 10 x 10 x 10 x 10, which equals 10,000. 6.9 ÷ 10,000 = 0.00069. Another way to think of this problem is to move the decimal in 6.9 to the left (because it is division) the number of places equal to the exponent (4).
3	B	The decimal point is being moved to the left, so it is a division problem. Since it is being moved 7 places, 8.2 is being divided by 10^7.
4	B	10^5 means 10 x 10 x 10 x 10 x 10, which equals 100,000. To find the number that is 100,000 times greater than 0.016, multiply 0.016 x 100,000, or move the decimal point to the right (because it is multiplication) the same number of places as the exponent (5).
5	10^3	To write a multiple of ten as a power of ten, count the number of zeros. Then express the quantity as ten to the power of the number of zeros. 1,000 has three zeros so, as a power of ten, 1,000 = 10^3

5.NBT.A.3.A Read and Write Decimals

Question No.	Answer	Detailed Explanations
1	B	In the number 0.05, the 5 is in the hundredths place. To show this amount (five hundredths) as a fraction, use 5 as the numerator and 100 as the denominator.
2	D	One half is equal to five tenths (think of a pizza sliced into 10 pieces, half of the pizza would be 5 out of 10 slices). To show five tenths, use a 5 in the tenths place immediately to the right of the decimal.
3	A	Sixty hundredths is equivalent to six tenths (the place to the right of the decimal). Three hundredths is shown by a 3 in the hundredths place (two places to the right of the decimal).
4	C	Begin by saying the whole number (forty), the word 'and' for the decimal, and then the decimal portion of the number. The decimal .057 is fifty-seven thousandths. The 5 hundredths is equivalent to fifty thousandths.
5	79,417,608	The millions (79) are separated from the thousands (417) by a comma. Another comma separates the thousands from the hundreds (608). The first option has the correct place values but contains a number reversal on seventeen thousand.

5.NBT.A.3.B Comparing & Ordering Decimals

Question No.	Answer	Detailed Explanations
1	B	In order to compare the size of numbers, begin with the place value furthest to the left. In this case, all of the numbers have a 2 in the ones place, so look to the tenths place to compare them. The number with the highest digit in the tenths place will come first (2.<u>4</u>). The next two highest numbers both have a 2 in the tenths place, so look to the hundredths place. The number with the highest digit in the hundredths place will come first (2.2<u>1</u>) followed by the number with the lower digit in the hundredths place (2.2<u>0</u>). The final number has a 0 in the tenths place, so it is the least of all.
2	A	The missing number must be greater than 4.17 but less than 4.19. Since the ones place (4) and tenths place (1) are the same, the missing number will begin with 4.1 as well. Looking to the hundredths place, the missing number must fall between 7 and 9. That makes it 4.18.

Question No.	Answer	Detailed Explanations
3	D	To compare these numbers, look at the digit in the highest place value (the tenths place). 0.<u>4</u>03 is greater than 0.<u>3</u>04 and 0.<u>0</u>43, as it has 4 in tenths place and the other two numbers have 3 and 0 in the tenths place respectively. Therefore options (A) and (B) are correct. In Option (C), we are comparing 0.<u>0</u>43 with 0.<u>3</u>04. 0.<u>3</u>04 has 3 in tenths place and 0.<u>0</u>43 has 0 in tenths place. Since 0 < 3, 0.043 < 0.304. So, option (C) is also correct. So, option (D) is the correct answer.
4	D	This pattern is increasing by one thousandth every term. After 2.039, the thousandth place will increase by one. Since there is already a 9 in the thousandth place, it will become zero and the hundredths place will increase to 4. The number 2.040 can also be written 2.04.
5	0.85 0.853 0.921 0.96 1.003 1.03	When comparing decimals, if the numbers do not have the same number of decimal places, add zeros to the end of the number until all numbers have the same number of decimals. Then compare the numbers ignoring the decimal point. 1.003, 0.853, 0.850, 1.030, 0.960, 0.921 – Now all numbers have three decimal points. 1003, 853, 850, 1030, 960, 921 – Ignore the decimal points. 850, 853, 921, 960, 1003, 1030 – Ordered from least to greatest 0.85, 0.853, 0.921, 0.96, 1.003, 1.03 – Decimals ordered from least to greatest

5.NBT.A.4 Rounding Decimals

Question No.	Answer	Detailed Explanations
1	D	In order for a number to round to 13.75, it must be between 13.745 and 13.754. The number 13.747 has a 7 in the thousandths place that means it will round up to 13.75.
2	B	Round $5.91 up to $6. Round $7.27 down to $7. Round $12.60 up to $13. $6 + $7 + $13 = $26.
3	C	Round 6.21 up to 7 and 2.5 up to 3. She needs two 7 feet pieces (=14 feet) and one 3 feet piece. She will have to buy about 17 feet (14 + 3) of wood.

Question No.	Answer	Detailed Explanations
4	A	Round each measurement to the nearest whole number, then multiply. 12.2 rounds down to 12 (because of the 2 in the tenths place) and 7.8 rounds up to 8 (because of the 8 in the tenths place). 12 x 8 = 96.
5		

	Round Up	Keep
Round 5.483 to the nearest hundredth.	○	●
Round 6.625 to the nearest tenth.	○	●
Round 77.951 to the nearest one.	●	○
Round 172.648 to the nearest hundredth.	●	○

When rounding, look at the digit to the right of the place to be rounded. If the digit is 5 or more, round to the next digit and drop the digits to the right. If the digit is less than 5, keep the number and drop the digits to the right.

A. When rounding 5.483 to the nearest hundredth, look at the thousands digit. Since the thousandths digit is 3, keep the hundredths digit and drop the numbers to the right. 5.483 rounded to the nearest hundredth is 5.48. KEEP

B. When rounding 6.625 to the nearest tenth, look at the hundredths digit. Since the hundredths digit is 2, keep the tenths digit and drop the numbers to the right. 6.625 rounded to the nearest tenth is 6.6. KEEP

C. When rounding 77.951 to the nearest one, look at the tenths digit. Since the tenths digit is 9, round the ones digit up to 8 and drop the numbers to the right. 77.951 rounded to the nearest one is 78. ROUND UP

D. When rounding 172.648 to the nearest hundredth, look at the thousandths digit. Since the thousandths digit is 8, round the hundredths digit up to 5 and drop the numbers to the right. 172.648 rounded to the nearest hundredth is 172.65. ROUND UP

5.NBT.B.5 Multiplication of Whole Numbers

Question No.	Answer	Detailed Explanations
1	D	The array shows three rows with seven objects in each row. There are 21 objects in all. The array is called a 3 by 7 array, which is shown as 3 x 7 = 21.
2	B	According to the Distributive Property of Multiplication, you can break one of the factors (101) into two parts (100 and 1) and multiply them both by the other factor. 596 x 100 and 596 x 1 will produce the same answer as multiplying 596 x 100 and adding 596 more.

Question No.	Answer	Detailed Explanations
3	C	Three of the trays held 15 cookies each, so 3 x 15 = 45. The other six trays held 18 cookies each, so 6 x 18 = 108. To find the total, add 45 + 108 = 153.
| 4 | B | ``` 
    4 0 7
  x 3 5
  _____
      3 5
       0
  2 0 0 0
    2 1 0
       0
+ 1 2 0 0 0
  _____
  1 4,2 4 5
``` |
| 5 | 595,134 | 321
× 1854
1284   321 x 4
16050   321 x 50
256800   321 x 800
321000   321 × 1000
595,134 |
```

5.NBT.B.6 Division of Whole Numbers

Question No.	Answer	Detailed Explanations
1	C	Divide the number of students by the number of seats in each row. 96 ÷ 10 = 9 R 6. The remaining 6 students still had to sit in a row, even though it was not full. The answer is 10 rows.
| 2 | C | 6720 divided by 15 is 448 with remainder 0 = 448 R 0 = 448 $\frac{0}{15}$<br><br>**Show Work:**<br><br>```
    0 4 4 8
1 5)6 7 2 0
    0
    6 7
    6 0
      7 2
      6 0
      1 2 0
      1 2 0
          0
``` |
3	D	To divide by 100, move the decimal point two places to the left. When a whole number ending with zeroes is the dividend, take off as many 0's as appear in the divisor from the dividend to get the quotient.
4	D	There is no number that can be divided by zero.
5	25 R 13	Start by dividing the 300 by 15. If 15 x 2 = 30, then 15 x 20 = 300. There are 20 fifteens in 300. The 88 will not divide evenly by 15, but 75 will (15 x 5 = 75). That gives us 25 x 15 = 375. Use this total to determine the remainder (388 - 375 = 13). The answer is 25 R 13.
```

5.NBT.B.7 Add, Subtract, Multiply, & Divide Decimals

Question No.	Answer	Detailed Explanations
1	B	Subtract the numbers, keeping their place values in line. Bring the decimal straight down to the solution. 0 9 11 12 1̶ 0̶ 2̶.2̶ - 9 8.6 ——————— 0 0 3.6
2	C	To solve, multiply without decimals. Then insert the decimal in your answer. Be sure the product has as many places to the right of the decimal as both factors. $ 0.4 2 x 8 ——— 1 6 + 3 2 0 ——— $ 3.3 6
3	B	To solve, multiply without decimals. Then insert the decimal in your answer. Be sure the product has as many places to the right of the decimal as both factors. 0.2 5 x 1.1 ——— 5 2 0 5 0 2 0 0 ——— 0.2 7 5
4	C	To solve, use division. Divide the numbers without the decimal point. Then, insert a decimal into the answer, leaving the same number of places to the right of the decimal as the dividend. 42 ÷ 3 = 14 --> 0.14
5	0.25	To solve, use division. Move both decimal places to the right one place, so you are dividing by a whole number (0.5 ÷ 2). Since 5 will not divide evenly by 2, think of it as 0.50. Divide the numbers without the decimal point. Then, insert a decimal into the answer, leaving the same number of places to the right of the decimal as the dividend (remember that you used 0.50, so there should be two places to the right of the decimal in your answer). 50 ÷ 2 = 25 →0.25

Number & Operations
- Fractions

5.NF.A.1 Add & Subtract Fractions

1. To add the fractions $\dfrac{3}{4}$ and $\dfrac{7}{12}$, what must first be done?

    A Reduce the fractions to lowest terms
    B Change to improper fractions
    C Make the numerators the same
    D Find a common denominator

2. Add: $\dfrac{1}{2} + \dfrac{1}{4} =$

    A $\dfrac{2}{6}$
    B $\dfrac{2}{3}$
    C $\dfrac{3}{4}$
    D $\dfrac{1}{2}$

3. Find the difference: $\dfrac{2}{3} - \dfrac{1}{9} =$

    A $\dfrac{1}{6}$
    B $\dfrac{5}{9}$
    C $\dfrac{3}{12}$
    D $\dfrac{2}{27}$

4. Find the sum: $2\dfrac{1}{8} + 5\dfrac{1}{2} =$

    A $7\dfrac{2}{10}$
    B $10\dfrac{1}{16}$
    C $3\dfrac{1}{6}$
    D $7\dfrac{5}{8}$

5. What is the value of $\dfrac{3}{5} - \dfrac{2}{7}$

    Write your answer in the box given below

5.NF.A.2 Problem Solving with Fractions

1. There were 20 pumpkins in a garden. One fourth of the pumpkins were too small, one tenth were too large, and one half were just the right size. The rest were not ripe yet. How many of the pumpkins were too small?

   Ⓐ 3
   Ⓑ 2
   Ⓒ 5
   Ⓓ 10

2. Timothy decided to clean out his closet by donating some of his 45 button-down shirts. He gave away 9 shirts. What fraction of the shirts did he give away?

   Ⓐ $\dfrac{1}{5}$

   Ⓑ $\dfrac{1}{9}$

   Ⓒ $\dfrac{1}{2}$

   Ⓓ $\dfrac{36}{45}$

3. There are 32 students in Mr. Duffy's class. If 4 come to after school tutoring, what fraction of the class comes to after school tutoring?

   Ⓐ $\dfrac{28}{32}$

   Ⓑ $\dfrac{1}{8}$

   Ⓒ $\dfrac{1}{4}$

   Ⓓ $\dfrac{2}{8}$

4. A 5th grade volleyball team scored 32 points in one game. Of those points, $\dfrac{2}{8}$ were scored in the second half. How many points were scored in the first half of the game?

   Ⓐ 12
   Ⓑ 4
   Ⓒ 20
   Ⓓ 24

5. Match the statement with the symbol that will make the statement true

	>	<	=
$\dfrac{5}{6} - \dfrac{2}{3} \ \square \ \dfrac{1}{2} - \dfrac{3}{8}$	◯	◯	◯
$\dfrac{5}{6} + \dfrac{2}{3} \ \square \ \dfrac{3}{4} + \dfrac{5}{12}$	◯	◯	◯
$\dfrac{3}{15} + \dfrac{2}{5} \ \square \ \dfrac{1}{3} + \dfrac{2}{5}$	◯	◯	◯
$\dfrac{7}{8} - \dfrac{1}{4} \ \square \ \dfrac{3}{4} - \dfrac{1}{8}$	◯	◯	◯

5.NF.B.3 Interpreting Fractions

1. If there are 90 minutes in a soccer game and 4 squads of players will share this time equally, how many minutes will each squad play?

   Ⓐ $\frac{22}{4}$

   Ⓑ $22\frac{1}{2}$

   Ⓒ $22\frac{2}{10}$

   Ⓓ $18\frac{4}{22}$

2. Damien has $695 in the bank. He wants to withdraw $\frac{2}{5}$th of his money. If he uses a calculator to figure out this amount, which buttons should he press?

   Ⓐ [6] [9] [5] [x] [2] [x] [5] [=]
   Ⓑ [6] [9] [5] [÷] [2] [x] [5] [=]
   Ⓒ [6] [9] [5] [÷] [2] [÷] [5] [=]
   Ⓓ [6] [9] [5] [x] [2] [÷] [5] [=]

3. Five friends are taking a trip in a car. They want to share the driving equally. If the trip takes 7 hours, how long should each friend drive?

   Ⓐ $\frac{5}{7}$ of an hour

   Ⓑ 1 hour 7 minutes

   Ⓒ $1\frac{2}{5}$ hours

   Ⓓ 1 hour 2 minutes

4. Which fraction is equivalent to 3 ÷ 10?

   Ⓐ $\frac{1}{3}$

   Ⓑ $\frac{10}{3}$

   Ⓒ $\frac{13}{3}$

   Ⓓ $\frac{3}{10}$

5. Justine found 6-feet of string with which to make 8 bracelets. If each bracelet was the same length, how long was each bracelet? Enter your answer in the box as a fraction in its simplest form.

```

```

5.NF.B.4 Multiply Fractions

1. Which of the following is equivalent to $\dfrac{5}{6} \times 7$?

   Ⓐ $5 \div (6 \times 7)$
   Ⓑ $(5 \times 7) \div 6$
   Ⓒ $(6 \times 7) \div 5$
   Ⓓ $(1 \div 7) \times (5 \div 6)$

2. Which of the following is equivalent to $\dfrac{4}{10} \times \dfrac{3}{8}$?

   Ⓐ $4 \div (10 \times 3) \div 8$
   Ⓑ $(4 + 3) \times (10 + 8)$
   Ⓒ $(4 \times 3) \div (10 \times 8)$
   Ⓓ $(4 - 3) \div (10 - 8)$

3. Hector is using wood to build a dog house. Each wall is $\dfrac{4}{7}$ of a yard tall and $\dfrac{3}{5}$ of a yard wide. Knowing that the area of each wall is the base times the height, how many square yards of wood will he need to build 4 walls of equal size?

   Ⓐ $1\dfrac{2}{3}$
   Ⓑ $1\dfrac{13}{35}$
   Ⓒ $\dfrac{12}{35}$
   Ⓓ $1\dfrac{4}{12}$

4. An auditorium has 600 seats. One-third of the seats are empty. How many seats are empty?

   Ⓐ 300 seats
   Ⓑ 400 seats
   Ⓒ 200 seats
   Ⓓ 900 seats

5. Fill in the table to complete the math sentence.

$\dfrac{1}{6}$	×		=	$\dfrac{3}{24}$	=	

5.NF.B.4.B Multiply to Find Area

1. **Lin and Tyra are measuring the area of the piece of paper shown below. Lin multiplied the length times the width to find an answer. Tyra traced the paper onto 1-inch graph paper and counted the number of squares. How should their answers compare?**

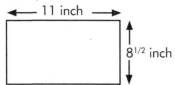

Ⓐ Lin's answer will be a mixed number, but Tyra's will be a whole number.
Ⓑ Tyra's answer will be greater than Lin's answer.
Ⓒ Lin's answer will be greater than Tyra's answer.
Ⓓ They should end up with almost exactly the same answer.

2. **Jeremy found that it takes 14 centimeter cubes to cover the surface of a rectangular image. Which of these measurements could possibly be the length and width of the rectangle he covered? Assume that centimeter cubes can be cut so that fractional measurements are possible.**

Ⓐ Length = $3\frac{1}{2}$ cm, width = 4 cm

Ⓑ Length = $4\frac{1}{2}$ cm, width = 3 cm

Ⓒ Length = 7 cm, width = 7 cm
Ⓓ Length = 7 cm, width = 3 cm

3. **What is the area of the court shown below?**

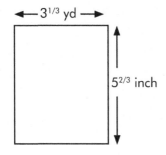

Ⓐ $15\frac{2}{9}$ yd²

Ⓑ $18\frac{8}{9}$ yd²

Ⓒ 16 yd²
Ⓓ 9 yd²

LumosLearning.com

4. **Find the area of the rectangle.**

$\frac{1}{2}$ m

$\frac{3}{4}$ m

5.NF.B.5.A Multiplication as Scaling

1. **If d * e = f, and e is a fraction less than 1, then f will be _____.**

    Ⓐ greater than d
    Ⓑ less than d
    Ⓒ equal to e ÷ d
    Ⓓ less than 1

2. **In which equation is r less than s?**

    Ⓐ r - 6 = s
    Ⓑ s * 6 = r
    Ⓒ r ÷ 6 = s

    Ⓓ s * $\dfrac{1}{6}$ = r

3. **Ryan and Alex are using beads to make necklaces. Ryan used one fifth as many beads as Alex. Which equation is true?**
   (Take R = Number of beads used by Ryan, A = Number of beads used by Alex).

    Ⓐ R * $\dfrac{1}{5}$ = A

    Ⓑ R = A * 5
    Ⓒ R * 5 = A
    Ⓓ R ÷ 5 = A

4. **Which statement is true about this equation?**
   5 x t = u

    Ⓐ t divided by u equals 5
    Ⓑ t plus 5 equals u
    Ⓒ u times 5 equals t
    Ⓓ t is $\dfrac{1}{5}$th of u

5. **Enter <1 or >1 into the table below to complete a true comparison.**

$\dfrac{8}{9}$	×		<	$\dfrac{8}{9}$
	×	$1\dfrac{1}{5}$	<	$1\dfrac{1}{5}$
$\dfrac{5}{4}$	×		>	$\dfrac{5}{4}$

5.NF.B.5.B Numbers Multiplied by Fractions

1. **Estimate the product:**

   $18{,}612 \times 1\dfrac{1}{7} =$ _____

   Ⓐ 11,000
   Ⓑ 17,000
   Ⓒ 36,000
   Ⓓ 21,000

2. **Which number completes the equation?**
   3,606 x ___ = 4,808
   Enter your answer in the box given below

3. **Which number completes the equation?**
   ___ $\times \dfrac{5}{6} = 17{,}365$

   Ⓐ 5,838
   Ⓑ 50,838
   Ⓒ 20,838
   Ⓓ 10,838

4. **When 6 is multiplied by the following fractions, which of the products will be greater than 6? Select all the correct answers.**

   Ⓐ $\dfrac{4}{5}$

   Ⓑ $\dfrac{10}{9}$

   Ⓒ $\dfrac{3}{2}$

   Ⓓ $\dfrac{13}{14}$

5.NF.B.6 Real World Problems with Fractions

1. There are $1\frac{4}{5}$ pounds of jelly beans in each bag. If Mrs. Lancer buys 3 bags of jelly beans for her class, how many pounds of jelly beans will she have in all?

   Ⓐ $3\frac{12}{15}$

   Ⓑ $5\frac{2}{5}$

   Ⓒ $3\frac{4}{15}$

   Ⓓ $5\frac{4}{5}$

2. Mario is in a bike race that is $3\frac{1}{5}$ miles long. He gets a flat tire $\frac{2}{3}$ of the way into the race. How many miles did he make it before he got a flat tire?

   Ⓐ $3\frac{2}{15}$

   Ⓑ $1\frac{3}{8}$

   Ⓒ $2\frac{2}{15}$

   Ⓓ $\frac{2}{3}$

3. Jackson is swimming laps in a pool that is $20\frac{1}{2}$ meters long. He swims $4\frac{1}{2}$ laps. How many meters did he swim?

   Ⓐ $80\frac{1}{4}$

   Ⓑ $92\frac{1}{4}$

   Ⓒ $84\frac{1}{2}$

   Ⓓ 90

4. Kendra ran 6 miles. Her friend Riley ran $\frac{2}{3}$ as far as Kendra. How far did Riley run? Simplify the answer and enter it in the box.

5.NF.B.7.A Dividing Fractions

1. Divide: $3 \div \dfrac{2}{3} =$

    Ⓐ $4\dfrac{2}{3}$

    Ⓑ $3\dfrac{2}{3}$

    Ⓒ 4

    Ⓓ $4\dfrac{1}{2}$

2. Complete the following:
    Dividing a number by a fraction less than 1 results in a quotient that is _____ the original number.

    Ⓐ the reciprocal of
    Ⓑ less than
    Ⓒ greater than
    Ⓓ equal to

3. 5 people want to evenly share a $\dfrac{1}{3}$ pound bag of peanuts. How many pounds should each person get?

    Ⓐ $\dfrac{3}{5}$

    Ⓑ $1\dfrac{2}{3}$

    Ⓒ $\dfrac{3}{15}$

    Ⓓ $\dfrac{1}{15}$

4. What four unit fractions complete the equations below? Enter your answers in the table.

2	÷		=	12
	÷	5	=	$\dfrac{1}{15}$
12	÷		=	48
	÷	4	=	$\dfrac{1}{28}$

5.NF.B.7.B Dividing by Unit Fractions

1. Which equation matches this model?

Ⓐ $24 \div \dfrac{1}{8} = 3$

Ⓑ $24 \div \dfrac{1}{3} = 8$

Ⓒ $8 \div \dfrac{1}{3} = 24$

Ⓓ $3 \div \dfrac{1}{8} = 24$

2. Byron has 5 pieces of wood from which to build his birdhouse. If he cuts each piece into fifths, how many pieces will he have?

Ⓐ 25

Ⓑ 5

Ⓒ $\dfrac{1}{5}$

Ⓓ $\dfrac{5}{25}$

3. Angelina has 10 yards of fabric. She needs $\dfrac{1}{3}$ yard of fabric for each purse she will sew. How many purses will she be able to make?

Ⓐ $3\dfrac{1}{3}$

Ⓑ $10\dfrac{1}{3}$

Ⓒ 30

Ⓓ 13

4. What three unit fractions complete the equations below? Enter your answers into the table.

	÷	14	=	$\dfrac{1}{112}$
	÷	29	=	$\dfrac{1}{87}$
	÷	55	=	$\dfrac{1}{495}$

5.NF.B.7.C Real World Problems Dividing Fractions

1. A team of 3 runners competes in a $\frac{1}{4}$ mile relay race. If each person runs an equal portion of the race, how far does each person run?

   Ⓐ $\frac{3}{7}$ mile

   Ⓑ $\frac{3}{12}$ mile

   Ⓒ $\frac{3}{4}$ mile

   Ⓓ $\frac{1}{12}$ mile

2. A beaker holds $\frac{1}{10}$ of a liter of water. If the water is divided equally into 6 test tubes, how much water will be in each test tube?

   Ⓐ $\frac{1}{60}$ liter

   Ⓑ $\frac{6}{10}$ liter

   Ⓒ $\frac{1}{6}$ liter

   Ⓓ $\frac{10}{16}$ liter

3. Mrs. Blake orders 3 pizzas for a school party. If each slice is $\frac{1}{12}$ of a pizza, how many slices are there in all?

   Ⓐ 24

   Ⓑ $4\frac{1}{3}$

   Ⓒ 36

   Ⓓ $\frac{3}{12}$

4. Mrs. Klein has a small rectangular area in her backyard to use for composting. If the width of the rectangular area is $1\frac{1}{7}$ yards and the compost area must be less than 6 square yards, what is the maximum length of the garden?
   Enter your answer in the box below.

Numbers and Operations – Fractions

Answer Key
&
Detailed Explanations

5.NF.A.1 Add & Subtract Fractions

Question No.	Answer	Detailed Explanations
1	D	Fractions must have a common denominator to be added. Multiply both the numerator and the denominator by 3 to get $\frac{9}{12}$ so that both the fractions have a common denominator 12.
2	C	Fractions must have a common denominator to be added. Multiply both the numerator and the denominator by 2 to get $\frac{2}{4}$. Then add the numerators (2+1) to get the numerator of the sum and keep the common denominator 4, to get the sum, $\frac{3}{4}$.
3	B	For subtracting fractions (proper or improper), find the common denominator and find the equivalent fractions in terms of this common denominator and subtract them. Then, write the fraction in its simplest form. $\frac{2}{3} = (2\times3)/(3\times3) = \frac{6}{9}$ $\frac{2}{3} - \frac{1}{9} = \frac{6}{9} - \frac{1}{9} = \frac{6-1}{9} = \frac{5}{9}$.
4	D	First add the whole numbers (2 + 5) to get 7. Then add the fraction parts. Since fractions must have a common denominator to be added, find the equivalent fractions in terms of the common denominator and add them. $\frac{1}{2}$ x (1x4)/(2x4) = $\frac{4}{8}$. $\frac{1}{8} + \frac{1}{2} = \frac{1}{8} + \frac{4}{8} = \frac{1+4}{8} = \frac{5}{8}$. The total is $7\frac{5}{8}$.
5	$\frac{11}{35}$	When subtracting fractions, first get a common denominator. The lowest common denominator of 5 and 7 is 5 X 7 = 35. Write an equivalent expression with denominators of 35 and subtract numerators. $\frac{3}{5} - \frac{2}{7} = \frac{21}{35} - \frac{10}{35} = \frac{11}{35}$

5.NF.A.2 Problem Solving with Fractions

Question No.	Answer	Detailed Explanations
1	C	This problem has a lot of extra information. To find the number of pumpkins that were too small, just multiply the total number of pumpkins (20) by the fraction of pumpkins that were too small ($\frac{1}{4}$). $20 \times \frac{1}{4} = \frac{20}{4}$ $= 5$ Convert from an improper fraction to a whole number by dividing 20 by 4.
2	A	Timothy gave away 9 out of 45 shirts. This is the fraction $\frac{9}{45}$. Since that option is not available, reduce the fraction to lowest terms by dividing both the numerator and denominator by 9. $\frac{9}{45} = \frac{9}{9} / \frac{45}{9} = \frac{1}{5}$
3	B	4 out of 32 students come to tutoring. This is the fraction $\frac{4}{32}$. Since that option is not available, reduce the fraction by dividing both the numerator and the denominator by 4. $\frac{4}{32} = (\frac{4}{4}) / (\frac{32}{4}) = \frac{1}{8}$
4	D	Multiply 32 by $\frac{2}{8}$ to find the number of points they scored in the second half. $32 \times \frac{2}{8} = \frac{64}{8} = 8$ If they scored 8 points in the second half, they must have scored 24 points in the first half (32 - 8 = 24).

Question No.	Answer	Detailed Explanations

5

	>	<	=
$\dfrac{5}{6} - \dfrac{2}{3} \; \square \; \dfrac{1}{2} - \dfrac{3}{8}$	◉	○	○
$\dfrac{5}{6} + \dfrac{2}{3} \; \square \; \dfrac{3}{4} + \dfrac{5}{12}$	◉	○	○
$\dfrac{3}{15} + \dfrac{2}{5} \; \square \; \dfrac{1}{3} + \dfrac{2}{5}$	○	◉	○
$\dfrac{7}{8} - \dfrac{1}{4} \; \square \; \dfrac{3}{4} - \dfrac{1}{8}$	○	○	◉

When adding or subtracting fractions first get a common denominator, then add or subtract the numerators and simplify the answer. When comparing fractions get a common denominator and compare numerators.

$$\dfrac{5}{6} - \dfrac{2}{3} = \dfrac{5}{6} - \dfrac{4}{6} = \dfrac{1}{6} \; ; \; \dfrac{1}{2} - \dfrac{3}{8} = \dfrac{4}{8} - \dfrac{3}{8} =$$

$$\dfrac{1}{8} \rightarrow \dfrac{1}{6} > \dfrac{1}{8} \text{ because } \dfrac{8}{48} > \dfrac{6}{48}$$

$$\dfrac{5}{6} + \dfrac{2}{3} = \dfrac{5}{6} + \dfrac{4}{6} = \dfrac{9}{6} = \dfrac{3}{2} \; ; \; \dfrac{3}{4} + \dfrac{5}{12} = \dfrac{9}{12} + \dfrac{5}{12}$$

$$= \dfrac{14}{12} = \dfrac{7}{6} \rightarrow \dfrac{3}{2} > \dfrac{7}{6} \text{ because } \dfrac{9}{6} > \dfrac{7}{6}$$

$$\dfrac{3}{15} + \dfrac{2}{5} = \dfrac{3}{15} + \dfrac{6}{15} = \dfrac{9}{15} = \dfrac{3}{5} \; ; \; \dfrac{1}{3} + \dfrac{3}{5} = \dfrac{5}{15} + \dfrac{9}{15}$$

$$= \dfrac{14}{15} \rightarrow \dfrac{3}{5} < \dfrac{14}{15} \text{ because } \dfrac{9}{15} > \dfrac{14}{15}$$

$$\dfrac{7}{8} - \dfrac{1}{4} = \dfrac{7}{8} - \dfrac{2}{8} = \dfrac{5}{8} \; ; \; \dfrac{3}{4} - \dfrac{1}{8} = \dfrac{6}{8} - \dfrac{1}{8}$$

$$= \dfrac{5}{8} \rightarrow \dfrac{5}{8} = \dfrac{5}{8}$$

5.NF.B.3 Interpreting Fractions

Question No.	Answer	Detailed Explanations
1	B	To solve, divide 90 minutes by 4 squads. This creates the improper fraction $\frac{90}{4}$. To change it to a mixed number, divide 90 by 4 to get 22 remainder 2. The remainder of 2 also needs to be divided among the 4 squads, so it becomes the fraction $\frac{2}{4}$, or $\frac{1}{2}$. Each squad will play for $22\frac{1}{2}$ minutes.
2	D	To find $\frac{2}{5}$ of 695, multiply the whole number by the fraction. Since $\frac{2}{5}$ is really $2 \div 5$, this means you will multiply $695 \times 2 \div 5$.
3	C	7 hours divided by 5 people is the fraction $\frac{7}{5}$. Of this, $\frac{5}{5}$ equals one whole, leaving $\frac{2}{5}$ as a fraction. These $\frac{2}{5}$ are not 2 minutes, they are a fraction of an hour. The total time is $1\frac{2}{5}$.
4	D	A fraction is the division of the numerator by the denominator. The fraction $\frac{3}{10}$ is equivalent to $3 \div 10$.
5	$\frac{3}{4}$	Divide 6-feet by 8 or write $\frac{6}{8}$. Then simplify the fraction $$\frac{6}{8} = \frac{\frac{6}{2}}{\frac{8}{2}} = \frac{3}{4}$$ Therefore each bracelet was $\frac{3}{4}$-feet long.

5.NF.B.4 Multiply Fractions

Question No.	Answer	Detailed Explanations
1	B	Multiplying a fraction by a whole number is the same as multiplying the numerator by a whole number then dividing the product by the denominator.
2	C	The product of two fractions is equal to the product of the numerators divided by the product of the denominators.

Question No.	Answer	Detailed Explanations
3	B	To solve, multiply $\frac{4}{7}$ x $\frac{3}{5}$ x 4. Multiply the first two terms first: $\frac{4}{7}$ x $\frac{3}{5}$ = $\frac{12}{35}$ Then multiply this fraction by 4. Remember that the whole number 4 can be shown as the fraction $\frac{4}{1}$. $\frac{12}{35}$ x 4 = $\frac{48}{35}$ Since $\frac{35}{35}$ is 1 whole the fraction can be shown as the mixed number $1\frac{13}{35}$.
4	C	Multiply 600 by $\frac{1}{3}$ to find the number of seats that are empty. $\frac{600}{1}$ x $\frac{1}{3}$ = $\frac{600}{3}$ = 200
5		When multiplying fractions, multiply numerators and put it over the product of the denominators. Then simplify the fraction. <table><tr><td>$\frac{1}{6}$</td><td>×</td><td>$\frac{3}{4}$</td><td>=</td><td>$\frac{3}{24}$</td><td>=</td><td>$\frac{1}{8}$</td></tr></table>

5.NF.B.4.B Multiply to Find Area

Question No.	Answer	Detailed Explanations
1	D	Multiplying length x width of a rectangle and tiling the rectangle with unit squares are both accurate ways to determine area. Therefore, Lin and Tyra should both end up with the same answer, or nearly the same answer (since counting fractional parts of tiles isn't as precise as multiplying).
2	A	Multiplying length x width of a rectangle should produce the same number as filling the rectangle with unit squares. Therefore, multiply to find that $3\frac{1}{2}$ x 4 = $\frac{7}{2}$ x 4 = $\frac{7 \times 4}{2}$ = $\frac{28}{2}$ = 14
3	B	Find the area of the court by multiplying: $3\frac{1}{3}$ x $5\frac{2}{3}$ = $\frac{10}{3}$ x $\frac{17}{3}$ = $\frac{170}{9}$ = $18\frac{8}{9}$ yd^2

Question No.	Answer	Detailed Explanations
4	$\frac{3}{8}$	To find the area, we need to multiply $\frac{1}{2}$ x $\frac{3}{4}$ = $\frac{3}{8}$. Hence, answer choice B is the correct answer.

5.NF.B.5.A Multiplication as Scaling

Question No.	Answer	Detailed Explanations
1	B	When multiplying, if one factor is a fraction less than 1, the product will be less than the other factor.
2	D	When multiplying, if one factor is a fraction less than 1, the product will be less than the other factor.
3	C	If Ryan has $\frac{1}{5}$ as many beads as Alex, then Alex has five times as many beads as Ryan. The way to show this is by multiplying Ryan's beads by 5 to equal Alex's beads.
4	D	When multiplying two numbers (a and b), the product will be a times as much as b or b times as much as a.
5		A whole number or fraction multiplied by a fraction less than one results in a value less than the original number. A whole number or fraction multiplied by a fraction greater than one results in a value greater than the original number. A. Since the result is a number less than $\frac{8}{9}$, the fraction entered must be less than one. B. Since the result is a number less than $1\frac{1}{5}$, the fraction entered must be less than one. C. Since the result is a number greater than $\frac{5}{4}$, the fraction entered must be greater than one.

5.NF.B.5.B Numbers Multiplied by Fractions

Question No.	Answer	Detailed Explanations
1	D	Multiplying a number by a fraction greater than 1 will result in a product that is greater than the original number. Since the second factor is only $\frac{1}{7}$ more than one, the product will be just slightly greater than 18,612. The only other option that is greater than 18,612 (option C: 36,000) is more than twice the original number.
2	$\frac{4}{3}$	Multiplying a number by a fraction greater than 1 will result in a product that is greater than the original number. Since the product is only slightly greater than the original number, the other factor will be just slightly greater than 1. Therefore, $\frac{4}{3}$ (which is equal to $1\frac{1}{3}$) is the only option possible.
3	C	Multiplying a number by a fraction less than 1 will result in a product that is less than the original number. Since the fraction is only slightly less than 1, the other factor will be just slightly greater than 17,365. Therefore, 20,838 is the only option possible, as 50,838 is more than double the product.
4	B & C	When multiplying a whole number by a fraction, if the fraction is less than one, the product will be less than the whole number. If the fraction is greater than one, the product will be greater than the whole number. The fractions that are greater than one are $\frac{10}{9}$ and $\frac{3}{2}$. Therefore 6 times either of these fractions will result in a product greater than 6. The correct answer choices are B and C.

5.NF.B.6 Real World Problems with Fractions

Question No.	Answer	Detailed Explanations
1	B	To multiply a whole number by a mixed number, first change the whole number to a fraction ($\frac{3}{1}$) and change the mixed number to a fraction ($\frac{9}{5}$). Multiply numerators (3 x 9 = 27) to find the numerator and multiply denominators (1 x 5 = 5) to find the denominator. The improper fraction $\frac{27}{5}$ can be changed to the mixed number $5\frac{2}{5}$
2	C	To multiply a fraction by a mixed number, change the mixed number to a fraction ($\frac{16}{5}$). Multiply numerators (2 x 16 = 32) to find the numerator and multiply denominators (3 x 5 = 15) to find the denominator. The improper fraction $\frac{32}{15}$ can be changed to the mixed number $2\frac{2}{15}$.
3	B	To multiply a mixed number by a mixed number, change each mixed number to a fraction ($\frac{41}{2}$ and $\frac{9}{2}$). Multiply numerators (41 x 9 = 369) to find the numerator and multiply denominators (2 x 2 = 4) to find the denominator. The improper fraction $\frac{369}{4}$ can be changed to the mixed number $92\frac{1}{4}$.
4	4 miles	To find how far Riley ran, multiply 6 by $\frac{2}{3}$. When multiplying a whole number by a fraction rewrite the whole number as a fraction with a denominator of 1. Then multiply the numerators and denominators. Finally simplify the answer to a fraction in simplest form or a mixed number. $6 \times \frac{2}{3} = \frac{6}{1} \times \frac{2}{3} = \frac{12}{3} = 4$

5.NF.B.7.A Dividing Fractions

Question No.	Answer	Detailed Explanations
1	D	The first step in dividing by a fraction is to find its reciprocal, which is the reverse of its numerator and denominator. The fraction $\frac{2}{3}$ becomes $\frac{3}{2}$. Then solve by multiplying (use $\frac{3}{1}$ for the whole number 3): $\frac{3}{1} \times \frac{3}{2} = \frac{9}{2} = 4\frac{1}{2}$
2	C	Dividing by a number less than one causes the original number to become larger. When dividing by a fraction less than 1, multiplying by its reciprocal will create a situation in which you multiply by a larger number and divide by a smaller number, therefore increasing the size.
3	D	To divide $\frac{1}{3}$ by 5, multiply $\frac{1}{3}$ by the reciprocal of 5, which is $\frac{1}{5}$. $\frac{1}{3} \times \frac{1}{5} = \frac{1}{15}$.
4		When trying to find a divisor or dividend when working with fractions, rewrite the question as a multiplication question and then take the reciprocal of the second fraction. A. $2 \times 6 = 12 \rightarrow 2 \div \frac{1}{6} = 12$ B. $3 \times 5 = 15 \rightarrow \frac{1}{3} \div 5 = \frac{1}{15}$ C. $12 \times 4 = 48 \rightarrow 12 \div \frac{1}{4} = 48$ D. $7 \times 4 = 28 \rightarrow \frac{1}{7} \div 4 = \frac{1}{28}$

5.NF.B.7.B Dividing by Unit Fractions

Question No.	Answer	Detailed Explanations
1	D	The model shows each of three units divided into eighths, resulting in a total of 24 units. That is shown as $3 \div \frac{1}{8} = 24$. Although option C is a true statement, it does not represent the model.
2	A	To solve, divide the 5 pieces of wood into fifths: $5 \div \frac{1}{5} = 5 \times 5 = 25$
3	C	To solve, divide the 10 yards of fabric into thirds: $10 \div \frac{1}{3} = 10 \times 3 = 30$

Question No.	Answer	Detailed Explanations
4		When trying to find a divisor when working with fractions quotients, rewrite the question as a multiplication question. A. $\frac{1}{8} \times \frac{1}{14} = \frac{1}{112} \rightarrow \frac{1}{8} \div 14 = \frac{1}{112}$ B. $\frac{1}{3} \times \frac{1}{29} = \frac{1}{87} \rightarrow \frac{1}{3} \div 29 = \frac{1}{87}$ C. $\frac{1}{9} \times \frac{1}{55} = \frac{1}{495} \rightarrow \frac{1}{9} \div 55 = \frac{1}{495}$

5.NF.B.7.C Real World Problems Dividing Fractions

Question No.	Answer	Detailed Explanations
1	D	Divide $\frac{1}{4}$ mile by 3 to solve: $\frac{1}{4} \div 3 =$ $\frac{1}{4} \times \frac{1}{3} = \frac{1}{12}$
2	A	Divide $\frac{1}{10}$ liter by 6 to solve: $\frac{1}{10} \div 6 =$ $\frac{1}{10} \times \frac{1}{6} = \frac{1}{60}$
3	C	To solve, divide the 3 pizzas by $\frac{1}{12}$: $3 \div \frac{1}{12} =$ $3 \times 12 = 36$
4	$5\frac{1}{4}$	To determine the maximum length, divide 6 by $1\frac{1}{7}$. $6 \div 1\frac{1}{7} = 6 \div \frac{8}{7} = \frac{6}{1} \times \frac{7}{8} = \frac{42}{8} = 5\frac{2}{8} = 5\frac{1}{4}$ Maximum length of the garden is $5\frac{1}{4}$ yards.

Measurement and Data

5.MD.A.1 Converting Units of Measure

1. **Complete the following.**
   2.25 hours = _____ minutes

   Ⓐ 135
   Ⓑ 225
   Ⓒ 145
   Ⓓ 150

2. **The normal body temperature of a person in degrees Celsius is about _____.**

   Ⓐ 0 degrees Celsius
   Ⓑ 37 degrees Celsius
   Ⓒ 95 degrees Celsius
   Ⓓ 12 degrees Celsius

3. **There are 8 pints in a gallon. How many times greater is the volume of a gallon compared to a pint?**

   Ⓐ 8 times greater
   Ⓑ $\frac{1}{8}$ times greater
   Ⓒ twice as great
   Ⓓ $\frac{8}{10}$ as great

4. **Which of the following measures about 1 dm in length?**

   Ⓐ a car
   Ⓑ a new crayon
   Ⓒ a ladybug
   Ⓓ a football field

5. **A meter is 100 centimeters. If a track is 500 meters long. How long is the track in centimeters? Enter your answer in the box given below.**

5.MD.B.2 Representing and Interpreting Data

1. **A 5th grade science class is raising mealworms. The students measured the mealworms and recorded the lengths on this line plot.**

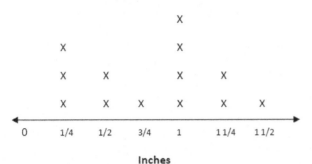

   According to this line plot, what was the most common length for mealworms?

   (A) $1\frac{1}{2}$ inches

   (B) $\frac{3}{4}$ inch

   (C) $\frac{1}{4}$ inch

   (D) 1 inch

2. **A 5th grade science class is raising mealworms. The students measured the mealworms and recorded the lengths on this line plot.**

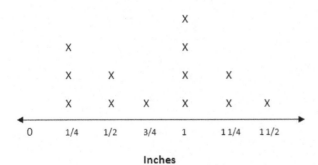

   According to this line plot, how many mealworms were less than 1 inch long?

   (A) 4
   (B) 6
   (C) 3
   (D) 2

3. A 5th grade science class is raising mealworms. The students measured the mealworms and recorded the lengths on this line plot.

Length of Mealworms

```
                              X

              X               X

              X      X        X       X

              X      X    X   X       X       X
        ◄─────┼──────┼──────┼──────┼──────┼──────┼──────►
        0    1/4    1/2    3/4    1    1 1/4  1 1/2
```

Inches

According to this line plot, how many mealworms were measured in all?

Ⓐ 4
Ⓑ 10
Ⓒ 13
Ⓓ $27\frac{3}{4}$

4. A 5th grade science class is raising mealworms. The students measured the mealworms and recorded the lengths on this line plot.

Length of Mealworms

```
                              X

              X               X

              X      X        X       X

              X      X    X   X       X       X
        ◄─────┼──────┼──────┼──────┼──────┼──────┼──────►
        0    1/4    1/2    3/4    1    1 1/4  1 1/2
```

Inches

According to this line plot, what is the median length of a mealworm?

Ⓐ 1 inch
Ⓑ 13 inches
Ⓒ between $\frac{3}{4}$ inch and 1 inch
Ⓓ $1\frac{1}{2}$ inches

5. The line plot below shows the weight in fractions of a gram for fifteen pieces of mail.
    How much does each piece of 3 mails next to $\frac{1}{2}$ gram weigh?

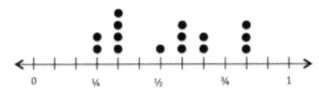

5.MD.C.3.A Volume

1. The volume of an object is the amount of _____.

    Ⓐ space it occupies
    Ⓑ dimensions it has
    Ⓒ layers you can put in it
    Ⓓ weight it can hold

2. Which of these could be filled with about 160 cubes of sugar if each sugar cube is one cubic centimeter?

    Ⓐ a ring box
    Ⓑ a moving box
    Ⓒ a cereal box
    Ⓓ a sandbox

3. Tony and Yolani are measuring the volume of a supply box at school. Tony uses a ruler to measure the box's length, width, and height in centimeters; then he multiplies these measurements. Yolani fills the box with centimeter cubes, then counts the number of cubes. How will their answers compare?

    Ⓐ They cannot be compared because they used different units.
    Ⓑ They will be almost or exactly the same.
    Ⓒ Tony's answer will be greater than Yolani's.
    Ⓓ Yolani's answer will be greater than Tony's.

4. Oscar wants to determine the volume of the chest, shown in the picture, in cubic inches. Complete the sentence below describing the dimensions of the unit cube.

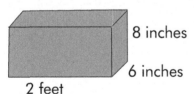

8 inches

6 inches

2 feet

Unit cube length	
Unit cube width	
Unit cube height	

5.MD.C.3.B Cubic Units

1. Which of these could possibly be the volume of a cereal box?

    Ⓐ 360 in³
    Ⓑ 520 sq cm
    Ⓒ 400 cubic feet
    Ⓓ 385 dm²

2. A container measures 4 inches wide, 6 inches long, and 10 inches high. How many 1 inch cubes will it hold?

    Ⓐ 20²
    Ⓑ 240
    Ⓒ The cube of 240
    Ⓓ Cannot be determined

3. Annie covers the bottom of a box with 6 centimeter cubes (A centimeter cube is a cube of dimensions 1 cm x 1 cm x 1 cm), leaving no gaps. If the volume of the box is 30 cm³, how many more centimeter cubes will she be able to fit inside?

    Ⓐ 5
    Ⓑ 180
    Ⓒ 24
    Ⓓ 4

4. What is the volume of the rectangular prism? Circle the correct answer choice.

    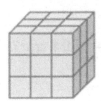   Key: ☐ represents one cubic unit

    Ⓐ 27 cubic units
    Ⓑ 18 cubic units
    Ⓒ 16 cubic units
    Ⓓ 21 cubic units

5.MD.C.4 Counting Cubic Units

1. Which of these has a volume of 24 cubic units?

 Ⓐ

 Ⓑ

 Ⓒ

 Ⓓ

2. Trevor is building a tower out of centimeter cubes. This is the base of the tower so far.

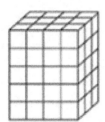

How many more layers must Trevor add to have a tower with a volume of 84 cm^3?

Ⓐ 7
Ⓑ 2
Ⓒ 5
Ⓓ 4

3. Kerry built the figure on the left and Milo built the one on the right. If they knock down their two figures to build one large one using all of the blocks, what will its volume be?

 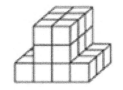

(A) 34 cubic units
(B) 16 cubic units
(C) 52 cubic units
(D) 40 cubic units

4. Use the picture of the solid below to complete the table. Write the numbers (only) in the blank spaces provided.

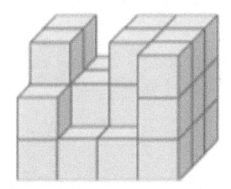

Number of cubes in the bottom layer	
Number of cubes in the middle layer	
Number of cubes in the top layer	
Volume of the solid	

5.MD.C.5.A Multiply to Find Volume

1. The figure has a volume of 66 ft³. What is the height of the figure?

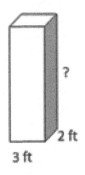

?
2 ft
3 ft

Ⓐ 11 ft
Ⓑ 61 ft
Ⓒ 13 ft
Ⓓ 33 ft

2. The figure has a volume of 14 cubic inches. What is the width of the figure?

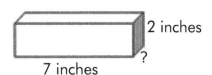

2 inches
?
7 inches

Ⓐ 2 inches
Ⓑ 1 inch
Ⓒ 5 inches
Ⓓ 2.5 inches

3. Which figure has a volume of 42 m³?

Ⓐ 3 m
2 m
6 m

Ⓑ 5 m
5 m
5 m

Ⓒ 9 m
2 m
4 m

Ⓓ 2 m
3 m
7 m

4. Piko filled a box with 4 layers of cubes that measured one foot on each side. If the bottom of the box fits 6 cubes, What is the volume of the box? Enter the answer in the box.

5.MD.C.5.B Real World Problems with Volume

1. A rectangular prism has a volume of 300 cm³. If the area of its base is 25 cm² how tall is the prism?

    Ⓐ 325 cm
    Ⓑ 7500 cm
    Ⓒ 12 cm
    Ⓓ 275 cm

2. Antonia wants to buy a jewelry box with the greatest volume. She measures the length, width, and height of four different jewelry boxes. Which one should she buy to have the greatest volume?

    Ⓐ 10 in x 7 in x 4 in
    Ⓑ 8 in x 5 in x 5 in
    Ⓒ 12 in x 5 in x 5 in
    Ⓓ 14 in x 2 in x 10 in

3. Damien is building a file cabinet that must hold 20 ft³. He has created a base for the cabinet that is 4 ft by 1 ft. How tall should he build the cabinet?

    Ⓐ 25 ft
    Ⓑ 20 ft
    Ⓒ 4 ft
    Ⓓ 5 ft

4. Bethany has a small rectangular garden that is 32 inches long by 14 inches wide. The average depth of the soil is 2 inches. If Bethany wanted to replace the soil, how much would she need? Circle the correct answer choice.

    Ⓐ 448 in³
    Ⓑ 896 in³
    Ⓒ 450 in³
    Ⓓ 48 in³

5.MD.C.5.C Adding Volumes

1. Ingrid is packing 1 foot square boxes into shipping crates. She has two shipping crates, shown below. How many boxes can she pack in them all together?

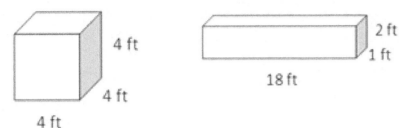

4 ft

4 ft

4 ft

2 ft

1 ft

18 ft

Ⓐ 64
Ⓑ 33
Ⓒ 82
Ⓓ 100

2. Bryson has two identical bookcases stacked one on top of the other. Together, they hold 48 ft³. If the area of the base is 8 ft², how tall is each bookcase?

Ⓐ 40 ft
Ⓑ 6 ft
Ⓒ 3 ft
Ⓓ 20 ft

3. Amy built a house for her gerbil out of two boxes. One box measures 6 cm by 3 cm by 10 cm and the other measures 4 cm by 2 cm by 2 cm. What is the total volume of the gerbil house?

Ⓐ 196 cm³
Ⓑ 180 cm³
Ⓒ 27 cm³
Ⓓ 2,880 cm³

4. A three-section warehouse holds a total of 24,766 ft³ of volume. The first section has a storage area of 436 ft² and a height of 19 ft. The second section has a height of 15 ft. and a depth of 26 ft. The volume of the first two sections is 17,254 ft³. Based on this information, complete the table below.

Volume of first section in cubic feet	
Length of the second section in feet	
Volume of the third section in cubic feet	

Measurement and Data

Answer Key
&
Detailed Explanations

5.MD.A.1 Converting Units of Measure

Question No.	Answer	Detailed Explanations
1	A	There are 60 minutes in each hour, so multiply: 2.25 x 60 300 1200 12000 135.00
2	B	At 0 degrees Celsius, water freezes. At 100 degrees Celsius, water boils. The only reasonable temperature for a human body is somewhere in between. The best estimate is 37 degrees Celsius.
3	A	8 pints=1 gallon, a gallon is 8 times greater in volume than a pint.
4	B	The prefix deci means ten. One dm (decimeter) is 10 centimeters in length. Option B is the correct answer. A crayon measures approximately 10 cms or 1 dm. Car and football field are very big and hence, options A and D are not correct. A Ladybug approximately measures 1 cm and hence, Option C is also incorrect.
5	50,000 cm	If 1 meter is 100 centimeters then there are 100 centimeters in one meter. So if the track is 500 meters long it is 500 x 100= 50,000 centimeters long.

5.MD.B.2 Representing and Interpreting Data

Question No.	Answer	Detailed Explanations
1	D	The Xs on the line plot represent the number of mealworms at each length. Since 1 inch has the most Xs above it (4), it is the most common length.
2	B	The Xs on the line plot represent the number of mealworms at each length. There were 3 mealworms that were $\frac{1}{4}$ inch long, 2 that were $\frac{1}{2}$ inch long, and 1 that was $\frac{3}{4}$ inch long. Altogether, that's 6 mealworms that are less than 1 inch long.
3	C	The Xs on the line plot represent the number of mealworms at each length. There are 13 Xs in all, at various lengths.
4	C	**Rule:** If the number data are odd, there will be one middle number which will be the median. If the number of data are even, there will be two middle numbers and the average of these numbers gives the median of the data set. The median value would be between 3/4 inch and 1 inch because the number of data is 6.

Question No.	Answer	Detailed Explanations
5	$\frac{7}{12}$	There are twelve divisions between 0 and 1. Thus distance between two successive divisions represents $\frac{1}{12}$ of a gram. Therefore the seventh division line represents $\frac{7}{12}$. There are three dots above this division to represent three pieces of mail. Therefore the correct answer is $\frac{7}{12}$.

5.MD.C.3.A Volume

Question No.	Answer	Detailed Explanations
1	A	Volume is a measurement of the space an object occupies. It is measured in cubic units.
2	C	The formula for determining volume is l x w x h. A cereal box could be about 8 cm x 2 cm x 10 cm, which is 160 cm³.
3	B	The formula for determining volume is l x w x h. It can also be determined by counting the number of unit cubes that fill a solid figure. Since Tony and Yolani both used centimeters as their units, their two methods should give them almost the same answer.
4	1,1,1	Unit cube length — 1; Unit cube width — 1; Unit cube height — 1. Because Oscar wants to determine the volume in cubic inches he should use a cube that represents a cubic inch. Such a cube would be 1 inch by 1 inch by 1 inch.

5.MD.C.3.B Cubic Units

Question No.	Answer	Detailed Explanations
1	A	This is the best option because not only is the value reasonable (a cereal box could measure 3 in x 10 in x 12 in, for example), but it also uses units appropriate for measuring volume.
2	B	The volume of the container is 240 in³ (4 x 6 x 10). That means it can hold 240 1-inch cubes.
3	C	If the volume of the box is 30 cm³, it can hold 30 centimeter cubes. Since there are already 6 in the box, there is room for 24 more (30 − 6 = 24).

Question No.	Answer	Detailed Explanations
4	A	To determine the volume of the rectangular prism, count the number of cubes. Each layer has 9 cubes and there are three layers so 9 X 3 = 27 cubes. The volume of the prism is 27 cubic units, choice A.

5.MD.C.4 Counting Cubic Units

Question No.	Answer	Detailed Explanations
1	D	By counting the number of cubes in the figure, you can find that the volume is 24 units^3. The bottom layer is 4 by 3 units, so it has a volume of 12 units^3. Each of the top 2 layers is 2 by 3 units, so they each have a volume of 6 units^3. Therefore, 12 + 6 + 6 = 24 units^3.
2	B	The base of the tower measures 4 x 3 x 5, which gives it a volume of 60 cm^3. Since each layer is 4 x 3, it has a volume of 12 cm^3. In order to reach 84 cm^3, Trevor must add 2 more layers (2 x 12 = 24 and 24 + 60 = 84).
3	D	Kerry's figure has a volume of 16 cubic units (you can see 8 cubes at the front of the figure and there are another 8 behind). Trevor's figure has a volume of 24 cubic units (The bottom layer is 4 by 3 units, so it has a volume of 12 units^3. Each of the top 2 layers is 2 by 3 units, so they each have a volume of 6 units^3. Therefore, the volume of Milo's figure is 12 + 6 + 6 = 24 units^3.) Together, their tower's volume is 40 cubic units (16 + 24 = 40).
4		Number of cubes in the bottom layer 12 Number of cubes in the middle layer 10 Number of cubes in the top layer 7 The volume of the solid is the sum of the cubes, which is 29.

5.MD.C.5.A Multiply to Find Volume

Question No.	Answer	Detailed Explanations
1	A	Since the volume (66 ft^3) must equal length x width x height, then 2 x 3 x 11 = 66.
2	B	Since the volume (14 in^3) must equal length x width x height, then 7 x 1 x 2 = 14.
3	D	To find the volume of a rectangular prism, multiply the length x width x height (7 x 3 x 2 = 42).
4	24	The volume of the box is equal to the number of cubes that will fit in the box. If six cubes fit on the bottom and there were four layers, the number of cubes is 6 X 4 = 24. Since each cube was 1 foot on each side or volume = 1 cubic feet, the volume of the box is 24 cubic feet.

5.MD.C.5.B Real World Problems with Volume

Question No.	Answer	Detailed Explanations
1	C	The volume of the container (300 cm^3) is equal to the area of the base (25) times its height. Therefore, 300 = 25 x 12.
2	C	To find the volume of a rectangular prism, multiply the length x width x height (12 x 5 x 5 = 300). This is greater than the other three jewelry boxes: 10 x 7 x 4 = 280 8 x 5 x 5 = 200 14 x 2 x 10 = 280
3	D	The volume of the cabinet (20 ft^3) will be equal to the area of the base (4 x 1 = 4) times its height. Therefore, the height should be 5 ft (20 = 4 x 5).
4	B	To determine the amount of soil Bethany would need, find the volume of the garden. Volume = l × w × h = 32 × 14 × 2 = 896 in^3.

5.MD.C.5.C Adding Volumes

Question No.	Answer	Detailed Explanations
1	D	To find the total volume (the number of cubes she can pack), add the volume of the first crate (4 x 4 x 4 = 64) to the volume of the second crate (18 x 2 x 1 = 36). 64 + 36 = 100
2	C	Since V = b x h, the bookcases must be 6 ft tall together (48 = 8 x 6). Therefore, each bookcase must be 3 ft tall (3 + 3 = 6).
3	A	To find the total volume, add the volume of the first box (6 x 3 x 10 = 180) to the volume of the second box (4 x 2 x 2 = 16). 180 + 16 = 196
4		<table><tr><td>Volume of first section in cubic feet</td><td>8284</td></tr><tr><td>Length of the second section in feet</td><td>23</td></tr><tr><td>Volume of the third section in cubic feet</td><td>7512</td></tr></table> (1) Volume of first section = Area of the base x height = 436 x 19 = 8284 cubic feet.

Question No.	Answer	Detailed Explanations
4 cntd...		(2) To calculate the length of the second section, first we have to calculate its volume. Volume of the second section = Total volume of first and second section - volume of first section = 17254 - 8284 = 8970 cubic feet. Volume = length x depth x height. Therefore, length = volume / (depth x height) = $\dfrac{8970}{26 \times 15} = \dfrac{8970}{390} = 23$ feet. (3) Volume of third section = Total volume of the warehouse - (sum of volume of first and second section) = 24766 - 17254 = 7512 cubic feet.

Geometry

5.G.A.1 Coordinate Geometry

1. Locate Point P on the coordinate grid. Which of the following ordered pairs represents its position?

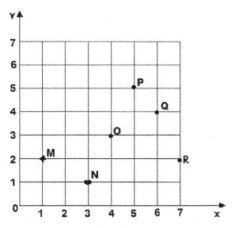

Ⓐ (5, 5)
Ⓑ (3, 1)
Ⓒ (1, 2)
Ⓓ (7, 2)

2. The graph below represents the values listed in the accompanying table, and their linear relationship. Use the graph and the table to respond to the following:
What is the value of c (in the table)?

X	Y
0	1
4	a
2	b
8	5
c	4

Ⓐ c = 9
Ⓑ c = 7
Ⓒ c = 6
Ⓓ c = 5

3. The graph below represents the values listed in the accompanying table, and their linear relationship. Use the graph and the table to respond to the following:
    What is the value of b (in the table)?

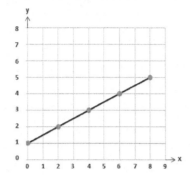

Ⓐ b = 1
Ⓑ b = 2
Ⓒ b = 3
Ⓓ b = 6

4. Which of the following graphs best represents the values in this table?

x	y
1	1
2	2
3	3

Ⓐ

Ⓑ

Ⓒ

Ⓓ

5. **Which of the following are the coordinates of points A, B and C? Circle the correct answer choice.**

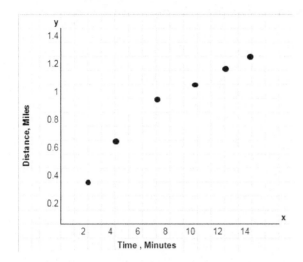

Ⓐ Point A: (2,6); Point B: (9,5); Point C: (6, 10)

Ⓑ Point A: (4,6); Point B: (12, 10); Point C: (18,5)

Ⓒ Point A: (4,6); Point B: (18, 5); Point C: (12,10)

Ⓓ Point A: (6,4); Point B: (10,12); Point C: (18,5)

5.G.A.2 Real World Graphing Problems

1. Which set of directions would lead a person from the playground (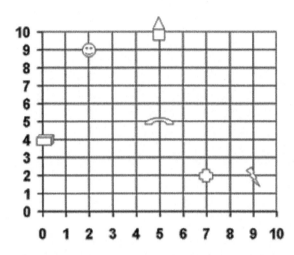) to the

    hospital ( )?

    (A) Walk 5 units along -ve y-axis and 7 units along +ve x-axis.
    (B) Walk 7 units along -ve y-axis and 2 units along +ve x-axis.
    (C) Walk 2 units along -ve y-axis and 7 units along +ve x-axis.
    (D) Walk 7 units along -ve y-axis and 5 units along +ve x-axis.

2. Which set of directions would lead a person from the weather station ( ) to the
    bridge ( )?

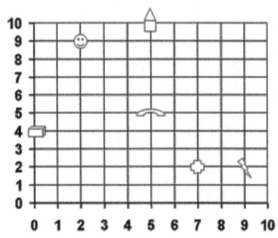

    (A) Walk 5 units along -ve x-axis and 5 units along +ve y-axis.
    (B) Walk 2 units along -ve x-axis and 0 units along +ve y-axis.
    (C) Walk 4 units along -ve x-axis and 3 units along +ve y-axis.
    (D) Walk 3 units along -ve x-axis and 4 units along +ve y-axis.

3. Where should the town locate a new lumber mill so it is as close as possible to both the warehouse (△) and the hospital (⊡)?

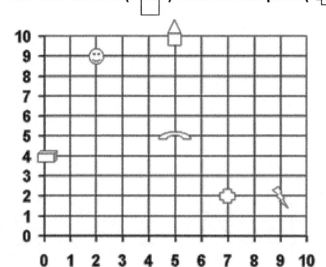

Ⓐ (7,0)
Ⓑ (5,3)
Ⓒ (1,7)
Ⓓ (5,0)

4. According to the map, what is the location of the zebras (🦓)?

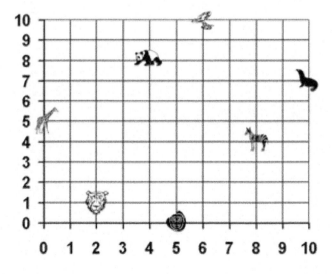

Ⓐ (8,4)
Ⓑ (8,0)
Ⓒ (4,8)
Ⓓ (4,4)

5. **During her run, Lui records the number of minutes it took to reach six-mile markers. Based on this graph, determine if the statements below are true or false.**

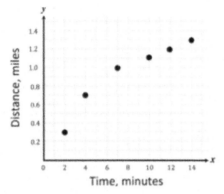

Time, minutes

	True	False
Lui reaches mile marker 1.0 in seven minutes.	○	○
It took Lui two minutes to run from mile marker 1.0 to mile marker 1.2.	○	○
Lui ran from mile marker 1.1 to mail marker 1.2 in three minutes.	○	○
Fourteen minutes after Lui started she reached mile marker 1.3.	○	○

5.G.B.3 Properties of 2D Shapes

1. **Complete the following.**
   This isosceles triangle has _____.

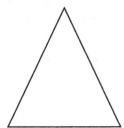

   Ⓐ one line of symmetry
   Ⓑ two congruent angles
   Ⓒ two equal sides
   Ⓓ all of the above

2. **Marcus used tape and drinking straws to build the outline of a two-dimensional shape. He used four straws in all. Exactly three of the straws were of equal length. What might Marcus have built?**

   Ⓐ a square
   Ⓑ a trapezoid
   Ⓒ a rectangle
   Ⓓ a rhombus

3. **How many pairs of parallel sides does a regular octagon have?**

   Ⓐ 8
   Ⓑ 4
   Ⓒ 2
   Ⓓ 0

4. **A rectangle can be described by all of the following terms except _____.**

   Ⓐ a parallelogram
   Ⓑ a polygon
   Ⓒ a prism
   Ⓓ a quadrilateral

5. Read the statements below and indicate whether they are true or false.

	True	False
All squares are rhombuses.	○	○
All parallelograms have four right angles.	○	○
All trapezoids have at least one set of parallel sides.	○	○
All squares are rectangles.	○	○

5.G.B.4 Classifying 2D Shapes

1. Which shape does not belong in section A of the diagram?

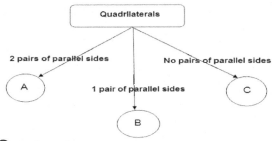

Ⓐ rectangle
Ⓑ trapezoid
Ⓒ rhombus
Ⓓ square

2. Which shape belongs in section A of the diagram?

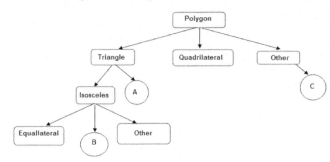

Ⓐ Scalene
Ⓑ Right
Ⓒ Acute
Ⓓ Symmetrical

3. Which shape belongs in section B of the diagram?

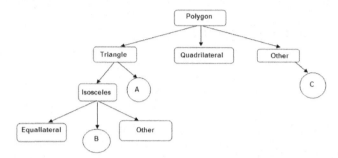

Ⓐ Scalene
Ⓑ Isosceles Right
Ⓒ Acute
Ⓓ Symmetrical

4. Which shape does not belong in section C of the diagram?

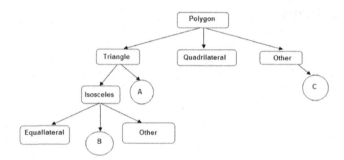

Ⓐ Octagon
Ⓑ Decagon
Ⓒ Pentagon
Ⓓ Rhombus

5. Which statement is true?

Ⓐ All triangles are quadrangles.
Ⓑ All polygons are hexagons.
Ⓒ All parallelograms are polygons.
Ⓓ All parallelograms are rectangles.

Geometry

Answer Key
&
Detailed Explanations

5.G.A.1 Coordinate Geometry

Question No.	Answer	Detailed Explanations
1	A	Using the labels, follow the x-axis as far as point P (5 units) and the y-axis as far as point P (5 units). This makes the coordinate pair (5, 5).
2	C	The coordinate pair is (c, 4), so follow the line on the graph to where its value for y is 4. Follow that point down to the x-axis to see it is 6.
3	B	The coordinate pair is (2, b), so follow the line on the graph to where its value for x is 2. Follow that point across to the y-axis to see it is 2.
4	B	As the value of x increases, the value of y increases equally. This produces an upward-sloping straight line.
5	C	Each point has coordinates (x-coordinate, y-coordinate). To determine the coordinates for each point, first determine the x-coordinate of the point and then the y-coordinate of the point. Be very careful to notice the interval of each division of the grid. This grid has a y-axis that increases by one for each division. The x-axis, however, increases by 2 for each division. Point A has an x-coordinate of 4 and a y-coordinate of 6 or (4,6). Point B has an x-coordinate of 18 and a y-coordinate of 5 or (18,5). Point C has an x-coordinate of 12 and a y-coordinate of 10 or (12,10). The correct answer choice is C.

5.G.A.2 Real World Graphing Problems

Question No.	Answer	Detailed Explanations
1	D	Starting at the playground (2,9), walking 7 units along the -ve y-axis could bring a person to (2,2). From there, walking 5 units along the +ve x-axis could bring that person to (7,2), to the location of the hospital.
2	C	Starting at the weather station (9,2), walking 4 units along the -ve x-axis could bring a person to (5,2). From there, walking 3 units along the +ve y-axis could bring that person to (5,5), to the location of the bridge.
3	B	This is the only set of coordinates given that is located between the warehouse and the hospital, making it the closest to both locations.
4	A	The location of the zebras is at the intersection of 8 on the x-axis and 4 on the y-axis. Therefore, its coordinates are (8,4).

5

	True	False
Lui reaches mile marker 1.0 in seven minutes. The x-coordinate associated with y = 1.0 is 7.	⬤	○
It took Lui two minutes to run from mile marker 1.0 to mile marker 1.2. Lui was at mile marker 1.0 at 7 minutes. She reached mile marker 1.2 at 12 minutes. Thus it took her 12-7 = 5 minutes to run from mile marker 1.0 to 1.2.	○	⬤
Lui ran from mile marker 1.1 to mail marker 1.2 in three minutes. Lui was at mile marker 1.1 at 10 minutes. She reached mile marker 1.2 at 12 minutes. Thus it took her 12-10 = 2 minutes to run from mile marker 1.1 to 1.2.	○	⬤
Fourteen minutes after Lui started she reached mile marker 1.3. The y-coordinate associated with x = 14 is 1.3.	⬤	○

5.G.B.3 Properties of 2D Shapes

Question No.	Answer	Detailed Explanations
1	D	By definition, an isosceles triangle has two equal sides and two congruent angles. It also has one line of symmetry (in this model, a vertical line through the center).
2	B	Marcus could not have made a square or a rhombus, since only three of the sides were of equal length. He also could not have made a rectangle, since the number of equal sides on a rectangle is either 2 or 4 (if it is a square). The shape he made must have been an (isosceles) trapezoid.
3	B	All of the opposite sides of a regular octagon are parallel. Since there are 8 sides, there are 4 pairs.
4	C	A prism is a 3-dimensional shape. Even though it can consist of rectangular faces, a rectangle is not a prism.
5		

	True	False
All squares are rhombuses.	◉	○
All parallelograms have four right angles.	○	◉
All trapezoids have at least one set of parallel sides.	◉	○
All squares are rectangles.	◉	○

(1) Since all sides of a square are equal, a square is also a rhombus. Therefore, the 1st statement is true.

(2) All parallelograms need not have four right angles. Therefore, the 2nd statement is false.

(3) A trapezoid has only one pair of parallel lines. Therefore, the 3rd statement is true.

(4) Each angle of a square measures 90 degrees. So, every square is also a rectangle. Therefore, the 4th statement is true.

5.G.B.4 Classifying 2D Shapes

Question No.	Answer	Detailed Explanations
1	B	A trapezoid is a quadrilateral which has only one pair of parallel sides.
2	A	Scalene is a type of triangle that is not isosceles.
3	B	An isosceles triangle can also be a right triangle (one with a 90° angle). Then it is called isosceles right triangle.
4	D	A rhombus has four sides, so it would fall under the heading quadrilateral in the hierarchy.
5	C	A polygon is a closed 2-dimensional figure made up of straight lines. Therefore, all parallelograms are polygons.

Additional Information

What if I buy more than one Lumos Study Program?

Step 1

Visit the URL and login to your account.
http://www.lumoslearning.com

Step 2

Click on 'My tedBooks' under the "Account" tab.
Place the Book Access Code and submit.

Step 3

To add the new book for a registered student, choose the
⦿ Existing Student button and select the student and submit.

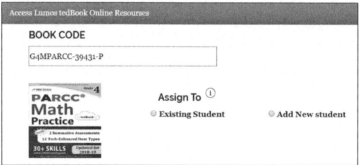

To add the new book for a new student, choose the ⦿ Add New student
button and complete the student registration.

Lumos StepUp® Mobile App FAQ For Students

What is the Lumos StepUp® App?

It is a FREE application you can download onto your Android Smartphones, tablets, iPhones, and iPads.

What are the Benefits of the StepUp® App?

This mobile application gives convenient access to Practice Tests, Common Core State Standards, Online Workbooks, and learning resources through your Smartphone and tablet computers.

- Eleven Technology enhanced question types in both MATH and ELA
- Sample questions for Arithmetic drills
- Standard specific sample questions
- Instant access to the Common Core State Standards
- Jokes and cartoons to make learning fun!

Do I Need the StepUp® App to Access Online Workbooks?

No, you can access Lumos StepUp® Online Workbooks through a personal computer. The StepUp® app simply enhances your learning experience and allows you to conveniently access StepUp® Online Workbooks and additional resources through your smartphone or tablet.

How can I Download the App?

Visit **lumoslearning.com/a/stepup-app** using your Smartphone or tablet and follow the instructions to download the app.

QR Code
for Smartphone
Or Tablet Users

Lumos StepUp® Mobile App FAQ For Parents and Teachers

What is the Lumos StepUp® App?

It is a free app that teachers can use to easily access real-time student activity information as well as assign learning resources to students. Parents can also use it to easily access school-related information such as homework assigned by teachers and PTA meetings. It can be downloaded onto smartphones and tablets from popular App Stores.

What are the Benefits of the Lumos StepUp® App?

It provides convenient access to

- Standards aligned learning resources for your students
- An easy to use Dashboard
- Student progress reports
- Active and inactive students in your classroom
- Professional development information
- Educational Blogs

How can I Download the App?

Visit **lumoslearning.com/a/stepup-app** using your Smartphone or tablet and follow the instructions to download the app.

**QR Code
for Smartphone
Or Tablet Users**

GRADE
5 »» 6

Developed by Expert Teachers

BACK TO SCHOOL
REFRESHER
ENGLISH
LANGUAGE ARTS

★ Grade 5 Review ★ Preview of Grade 6

Measure and Remediate Learning Loss

Diagnose Learning Gaps

Get Targeted Practice

Prepare for Grade 6

(((tedBook)))

Updated for 2021-22

Includes Additional Online Practice

Other Books By Lumos Learning For Grade 6

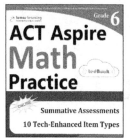 

ACT Aspire Math & ELA Practice Book

AzM2 Math & ELA Practice Book

CMAS Math & ELA Practice Book

FSA Math & ELA Practice Book

GMAS Math & ELA Practice Book

ILEARN Math & ELA Practice Book

IAR Math & ELA Practice Book

LEAP Math & ELA Practice Book

Other Books By Lumos Learning For Grade 6

MAAP Math & ELA Practice Book

MAP Math & ELA Practice Book

MCAS Math & ELA Practice Book

MCAP Math & ELA Practice Book

NYST Math & ELA Practice Book

NJSLA Math & ELA Practice Book

OST Math & ELA Practice Book

PARCC Math & ELA Practice Book

Other Books By Lumos Learning For Grade 6

SBAC Math & ELA Practice Book

STAAR Math & ELA Practice Book

TNReady Math & ELA Practice Book

Available
- At Leading book stores
- www.lumoslearning.com/a/lumostedbooks

Made in the USA
Las Vegas, NV
20 August 2021